# SHE'S ON THE MONEY

## ANDREA HALL

### ILLUSTRATED BY
## LI ZHANG

## ALBERT WHITMAN & COMPANY
## CHICAGO, ILLINOIS

To Lee, Paul, and Floyd—AH
For the girls who have dreams—LZ

Library of Congress Cataloging-in-Publication data is on file with the publisher.
Text copyright © 2021 by Andrea Hall
Illustrations copyright © 2021 by Albert Whitman & Company
Illustrations by Li Zhang
All coins and bills shown in this book are illustrated representations.
First published in the United States of America in 2021
by Albert Whitman & Company
ISBN 978-0-8075-7342-6 (hardcover)
ISBN 978-0-8075-7357-0 (ebook)

Design by Rick DeMonico

For more information about Albert Whitman & Company,
visit our website at www.albertwhitman.com.

# Introduction

Before money existed, people bartered, or exchanged, items. A basket could be exchanged for a pot, or salt exchanged for shells, or a cow exchanged for a sheep. People traded what they had for what they needed, giving items value.

In about 5000 BCE, pieces of metal, mainly gold and silver, were considered valuable, so people began using them to pay for goods. These pieces of metal were the first coins. But coins are heavy, making them difficult to carry around. So in about 950 CE, paper money was invented and first used in China.

Many coins and paper bills have images of people on them. Who are these people? And who chooses them?

Many nations choose their country's founders, political leaders, or others who have contributed to their country's success. Historically, the people chosen have primarily been men. However, some countries over the centuries have recognized the contributions of women. These women come from all different backgrounds. They are novelists, scientists, artists, and activists. Sometimes their accomplishments are in more than one field.

This book looks at how a few of these notable women were chosen to appear on money and gives a glimpse of what life was like when these women were alive. A number of these women overcame big challenges, and some fought to improve the lives of others. They weren't afraid to follow their own paths. Each of these women left a legacy.

# Cleopatra VII Thea Philopater

## Pharaoh of Egypt • Ruler of an Empire

| Born | about 69 BCE in Alexandria, Egypt |
|------|------------------------------------|
| Died | 30 BCE (39 years old) |

Cleopatra appears on currency because she put herself on it. As ruler of Egypt, she had her own coins minted, or made. Unlike many women that came after them, Egyptian women of Cleopatra's time could buy property, divorce and remarry, and serve on juries. And like Cleopatra, they could be rulers.

Cleopatra was eighteen when her father died and she became the Pharaoh of Egypt. At first, she was coruler with her ten-year-old brother. When his advisors tried to get rid of her, Cleopatra fled Alexandria.

She smuggled herself back into the royal palace in Alexandria a year later, rolled in a carpet—or according to some stories, a bedroll tied with a leather string. Cleopatra went to ask Julius Caesar, one of the Roman generals, for help. He was impressed and used his power to help her regain the throne.

We know from historical records that after her death Cleopatra was embalmed—a traditional Egyptian practice of removing all moisture from a body to preserve it—making her a mummy. But the location of her grave remains a mystery.

The silver denarius, issued by Cleopatra in 32 BCE, shows her image. It was worth about one day's minimum wage in Egypt at the time.

The Latin caption translates as "For Cleopatra, Queen of Kings and the children of Kings."

The reverse side shows Mark Antony, a Roman politician and general.

Cleopatra often wore a traditional Egyptian headdress made of linen. One headdress, called Nemes, was made of blue and gold striped cloth that covered the crown of the head and hung down to the shoulders.

Another headdress was the Khat, a single-colored cloth that covered the hair and was tied at the base of the head to form a tail. A metal headband held the cloth in place.

Cleopatra liked to dress in the style of the country where she was. When in Egypt, she wore a sheer dress and sandals with jewels. She also wore a lot of jewelry, including gold bands that looked like snakes on her upper arms and pearls in her hair.

The embalming process took seventy days. The organs were removed, preserved in special jars, and buried with the corpse, which was wrapped in hundreds of yards of linen.

Some animals, such as baboons, cats, birds, and crocodiles, were also mummified, sometimes because they were beloved pets.

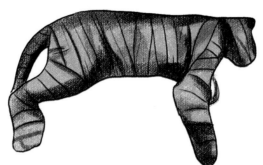

# Maria Sibylla Merian
## Entomologist • Scientific Illustrator

Maria Sibylla Merian was one of the first entomologists—people who study insects—and scientific illustrators. Her childhood was filled with books and art, and her stepfather taught her to paint. But Maria was bored with still-life portraits—she wanted to paint living things. Maria loved to watch butterflies and other insects, observing how they moved.

Maria's interest in bugs was unusual for her time. People believed that bugs were "evil spirits" because they came out of the ground. Maria thought that was silly. She captured bugs and the plant life where they were found and began drawing and painting them in secret. She had to keep her work quiet so she wasn't accused of being "evil." Through her study of caterpillars, she witnessed metamorphosis—the process of a caterpillar becoming a butterfly. Maria found the transformation fascinating, not scary.

| Born | April 2, 1647, in Frankfurt, Germany |
|------|--------------------------------------|
| Died | January 13, 1717, in Amsterdam, the Netherlands (69 years old) |

In her fifties, Maria traveled to Suriname, South America, on her first scientific expedition. She published her illustrations to share with the scientific community. Because of Maria, we know much more about plant and insect life in the jungle.

Maria published her books in German instead of Latin so regular people, not just scientists, could read them.

*Catasticta sibyllae*, a new butterfly species, was named for Maria in 2018.

Maria was featured on the 500-deutsche-mark banknote from October 27, 1992 to the end of 2001, when Germany began using the euro.

Behind Maria are historic buildings of Nuremberg, a city in Germany where she lived.

Color-shifting ink displays two different colors depending on the angle it is viewed. On the 500 DM, the lower half of the number on the front of the bill shifts from gold to green when tilted.

The back of the note shows a dandelion and the pale tussock moth in both its caterpillar and butterfly phases—two living things Maria liked to draw.

Maria and her artwork have been featured on stamps in Germany, Suriname, and the United States.

# Catherine Flon
## Seamstress • Revolutionary • Heroine

Catherine Flon sewed the first Haitian flag when the country won its independence from France in 1804. She was asked to sew the first flag by her godfather, Jean-Jacques Dessalines. He was the revolutionary leader who started a revolt to free Haiti from French rule, ending slavery in the country. Haiti became the first country founded by formerly enslaved people.

| Born | date unknown in Arcahaie, Haiti |
|------|--------------------------------|
| Died | unknown |

Little is known about Catherine's life. Very few enslaved people could read or write, so they were unable to document their history. There are no birth or death records in her name.

As one legend goes, Jean-Jacques tore apart the French flag and asked Catherine to put it back together without the white stripe. She had been taught to sew and had the knowledge and ability to put a new flag together. It's possible the blue and red stripes indicate the coming together of citizens of African descent and citizens of mixed European and African descent.

Catherine is featured on the ten-gourdes banknote first issued in 1988. She is the first woman to be honored on Haitian money.

Flag Day is celebrated on May 18 to commemorate the day Catherine finished the Haitian flag. The current flag, with the Haitian coat of arms, was adopted in 1986.

The reverse side of the note shows the Haitian coat of arms, first used in 1807. The motto is in French and translates to "union makes strength." The royal palm represents Haitian independence. The Phrygian cap, otherwise known as a liberty cap, is a common symbol of freedom.

Haiti makes up the western third of the island of Hispaniola. The other two-thirds of the island is the Dominican Republic, which became independent from Haiti in 1844.

Arcahaie, the town where Catherine was born, is nicknamed "flag town."

Women still dress up like Catherine during festivals and national holidays. Traditional clothing includes a short-sleeved blouse, colorful skirt, and a head scarf, all usually made of cotton or linen.

# Sacagawea
## Adventurer • Naturalist • Interpreter

A member of the Lemhi Shoshone tribe, Sacagawea is remembered for her role as a guide for the Lewis and Clark Expedition.

The daughter of a Shoshone chief, Sacagawea was kidnapped by the Hidatsa tribe when she was eleven or twelve. She was later sold or given (no one is sure) to a French-Canadian fur trader, Toussaint Charbonneau, as his wife.

In her mid-teens, Sacagawea was part of the Lewis and Clark Expedition to explore, map, and find a route to the Pacific Ocean.

| Born | about 1788 in the Salmon River region of what is now Idaho |
|------|-----------------------------------------------------------|
| Died | 1812 at Fort Manuel in what is now South Dakota (25 years old) |

Sacagawea was pregnant at the time and either gave birth a few months before the group set off or a few months into the expedition. She helped find plants to eat and to use as medicine. Having a Native woman and infant along also made the group seem more friendly to other Native tribes.

Sacagawea could help Lewis and Clark communicate with the other tribes because she spoke several Native languages. When the group came across the Shoshone tribe, Sacagawea discovered her brother was now the chief. Sacagawea was able to buy horses from him, which made the next phase of the expedition, through the mountains, possible.

"Amazing the things you find when you bother to search for them."
—Sacagawea

Sacagawea helped keep herself and others alive on the journey by finding edible plants, such as wild licorice.

Sacagawea was the only woman on the Lewis and Clark Expedition, which was named the "Corps of Discovery." This map shows what the country looked like at the time of the expedition.

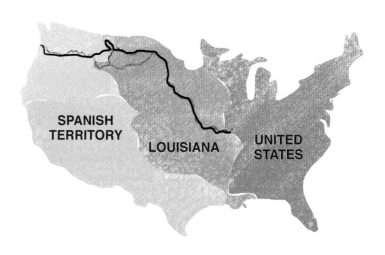

SPANISH TERRITORY

LOUISIANA

UNITED STATES

The Sacagawea dollar coin was issued in 2000.

Sacagawea is carrying her newborn son. Since no photos of Sacagawea exist, the designer, Glenna Goodacre, who also designed the Vietnam Women's Memorial in Washington, DC, used a modern Shoshone woman as a model.

Although gold in color, the coin is actually made up of copper, zinc, manganese, and nickel. The gold color helps the visually impaired tell the coins apart more easily—if someone is unable to make out the text on the coin, the color difference makes the coin recognizable. The plain, not ridged, edge also helps identify the coin.

All US coins are stamped with the words *E Pluribus Unum*, which is Latin for "Out of many, one."

The bald eagle is the US national bird. The seventeen stars symbolize each state in the Union at the time of the expedition.

Part of the trip was made by keelboat. One time the boat almost capsized, but Sacagawea was able to save documents and supplies.

# Jenny Lind

## Opera Singer • Educator • Celebrity

The official currency of Sweden is the krona, which means "crown."

Jenny was featured on the fifty-krona note issued in 1996. The musical notes on the bill are from the opera *Norma* by Vincenzo Bellini. Jenny sang the lead role in this opera in Germany. Stockholm's old opera house, where Jenny made her debut, is also featured.

Jenny Lind was a famous opera singer nicknamed the "Swedish Nightingale."

Raised by a single mother, Jenny grew up in poverty. She and her mother lived in shelters or with church friends. When Jenny was nine, an attendant to a principal dancer from the Swedish Royal Opera overheard her singing. The attendant told the dancer, who agreed Jenny's voice was special and got her an audition. Jenny was accepted into a training program and made her opera debut at eighteen.

When she was approached in 1849 by P.T. Barnum, an American entertainer and businessman, to do a US tour, Jenny saw it as an opportunity to choose her own program. She

| Born | Johanna Maria Lind on October 6, 1820, in Stockholm, Sweden |
|------|--------------------------------------------------------------|
| Died | November 2, 1887, in Malvern, England (67 years old) |

decided to sing popular songs in addition to opera pieces, since opera was relatively new to the United States in 1850. P.T. Barnum advertised her performances and made Jenny into a celebrity in the US. More than 30,000 people gathered at New York Harbor to greet Jenny when she arrived.

The reverse side shows a *nyckelharpa*, or silver harp, a traditional Swedish musical instrument. The musical notes indicate its tonal range.

**50** **50**

**FEMTIO KRONOR**

Jenny's image has appeared on candy tins, paper dolls, and figurines, among many other items while she was alive. "Lindomania" began in Europe but swept to the United States when Jenny arrived for her tour.

Jenny Lind
PETITE CHOCOLATES

Jenny chose to wear a simple white dress at her performances on the US tour.

A steam train built in England in 1847 was named after her.

# Kate Sheppard
## Suffragist • Writer • Public Speaker

Katherine "Kate" Sheppard was a leader of the women's rights movement in New Zealand. She helped make New Zealand the first country to give women the vote.

Kate moved to New Zealand in 1868, but she didn't start working for women's rights until almost twenty years later. In 1885 she joined the Women's Christian Temperance Union to fight for a ban on alcohol. The WCTU needed to win the right to vote for their voices to be heard.

In 1893 Kate helped organize a petition calling for women to get the right to vote. More than 32,000 signatures, from women and men, showed the nation was ready for change. Later that year, the Electoral Act passed, making New Zealand the first country to grant women the right to vote. It became an inspiration for women's rights movements all over the world.

| Born | Katherine Malcolm on March 10, 1848, in Liverpool, England |
|------|-------------------------------------------------------------|
| Died | July 13, 1934, in Christchurch, New Zealand (86 years old) |

Kate went on to fight for equal rights in marriage, to encourage physical activity and health in women, and to push for clothing that made exercise possible—which meant abolishing constricting corsets.

The bird in the lower left front corner changes from blue to green at different angles.

AA1 728459

Women in Sheppard's time were expected to wear corsets, undergarments that were sometimes tight and restricted movement.

In the 1890s many women began riding bicycles, which were invented in 1817. Changes to women's clothing were necessary to make riding bicycles easier and safer. The bicycle allowed women in New Zealand to travel greater distances to gather more signatures.

New Zealand's currency is called the dollar, just like US currency. Its nickname is the "kiwi" for the national bird. The kiwi is featured on the dollar coin.

Kate is featured on the ten-dollar bill issued in 1991 along with a white camellia. This flower was given to all members of parliament in 1893 who supported universal suffrage, or the right to vote.

There's a variety of the camellia flower named the Kate Sheppard.

**"Do not think your single vote does not matter much. The rain that refreshes the parched ground is made up of single drops."**

**—Kate Sheppard**

In the transparent window, the numbers, bird, and fern are all metallic.

Wildlife native to New Zealand is shown on the back of the bill: a blue duck, or whio; a kiokio fern; and a pineapple scrub.

# Maria Montessori

## Doctor • Teacher • Creative Thinker

Maria Montessori created her own method of educating young children. In Maria's family, education was important. Girls growing up in her time often didn't go to school, but Maria loved to learn and went to a boys' technical institute in Rome as a teen. She was initially rejected from medical school, but she studied hard and applied again. In 1896 she became one of the first female doctors in Italy.

Maria worked with children with developmental disabilities. She believed children should learn naturally through playing and exploring using their senses, so she developed a method of education built on that belief. Maria opened her first Montessori school in Rome on January 6, 1907. By 1910 Montessori schools could be found throughout Europe. The United States opened its first Montessori school in 1911. There are thousands of Montessori schools in the United States and around the world today.

| Born | August 31, 1870, in Chiaravalle, Italy |
|------|----------------------------------------|
| Died | May 6, 1952, in the Netherlands (81 years old) |

**"The greatest sign of success for a teacher... is to be able to say, 'The children are now working as if I did not exist.'"**

**—Maria Montessori**

Alexander Graham Bell, inventor of the telephone, and his wife opened a Montessori school in their home in Canada.

Maria and her Montessori schools have been featured on stamps in the Netherlands, Italy, India, the Maldives, Pakistan, and Sri Lanka.

**1000 LIRE MILLE**

FG 08G286 N

Antonio tazio

FG 086.86 N

Maria Montessori was shown on the 1,000-lira note in Italy. It was issued December 27, 1990.

The lira was the official currency of Italy until January 1, 1999, when Italy began using the euro.

The winged lion of Saint Mark is a symbol of the city of Venice.

The bill is printed on heavy cotton paper, or "rag paper," to make it easy to tell when bills are fake. Rag paper is not artificially bleached like commercial paper, and even ultraviolet light can't pass through it.

The puzzle pieces on the front and back of the bill refer to the Montessori method of education.

**1000**

Children teaching themselves is one of the principles of the Montessori method.

# Ichiyō Higuchi
## Writer • Poet • Realist

Ichiyō Higuchi was the first major woman writer during the Meiji era (1868–1912) of Japan. She wrote twenty-one short stories, two novels, and more than four thousand poems.

In Ichiyō's time, girls in Japan were only required to attend school for six years. After that, Ichiyō's father bought her books and hired a tutor to teach her at home. Her father was well educated, and he wanted Ichiyō to be too.

At age fourteen, she enrolled in Haginoya, a private school, where she studied poetry and classics. Ichiyō was at the top of her class.

But when Ichiyō was seventeen, her father died. The

| Born | Natsu Higuchi on May 2, 1872, in Tokyo, Japan |
|------|-----------------------------------------------|
| Died | November 23, 1896, in Tokyo, Japan (24 years old) |
| Pen name | Ichiyō (translates to "single leaf" in English) |

family was poor, so Ichiyō dropped out of school to take care of her mother and younger sister. She worked to make money by writing. Her stories stood apart because she wrote about the suffering of women in the lower classes. Exploring the harsh circumstances women faced without giving the stories happy endings made her the most important female writer of her time.

On the 5,000-yen note, the bottom two corners each contain an octagon that is an anti-counterfeiting measure.

**Tanka Poem by Ichiyō:**

Casually,
To see just your shadow,
I passed through
Your house's gate
Several times.

Tanka poetry: A short poem consisting of five lines or phrases, with the following syllabic units: 5-7-5-7-7. The English translation of Ichiyō's poem does not follow the pattern of syllables. A tanka poem is usually written to express feelings.

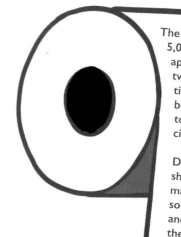

The life span of a 5,000-yen bill is approximately one to two years. After this time, the bills tend to be damaged and need to be removed from circulation and replaced.

Damaged bills are shredded and used to make housing materials, solid fuel, toilet paper, and office supplies, or they are incinerated as waste.

Ichiyō is featured on the front of the 5,000-yen note.
Date of issue: November 1, 2004.

She wears a kimono, the national dress of Japan. A kimono is generally made out of silk. The material is wrapped left over right and secured with a sash—there are no buttons or zippers.

The bills are made with ink applied more heavily in certain areas so that various spots feel different when touched, making it easier for people who are visually impaired to use the currency.

A watermark, a faint image or pattern created by using different thicknesses in the paper, of Ichiyō is in the center. The bill must be held up to light for the watermark to be visible.

The reverse side has a painting of irises by Ogata Kōrin, a Japanese painter, lacquerer, and designer. In Japan, irises are viewed as purifying and protective flowers.

# Helen Keller
## Educator • Advocate • Ambassador

Helen Keller advocated for others with disabilities like her own.

At age two, Helen contracted a disease that left her deaf, blind, and without a way to communicate. Her parents took her to many doctors, trying to find help. But it was a recent college graduate, Anne Sullivan, who finally communicated with Helen when she was six.

| Born | June 27, 1880, in Tuscumbia, Alabama |
|------|---------------------------------------|
| Died | June 1, 1968, in Easton, Connecticut, weeks shy of her 88th birthday |

Helen worked with Anne until Anne died in 1936. Helen learned to communicate through sign language and spent twenty-five years learning to speak. She worked hard and didn't let being deaf or blind stop her from going to school. She attended Radcliffe College from 1900 to 1904.

After graduating, Helen wanted to help others like herself. She spoke to Congress about improving aid for people who are blind. In 1915 Helen also cofounded Helen Keller International, a nonprofit organization to reduce causes of blindness around the world. She first started the group to help soldiers who became blind in World War I. Later, Helen Keller International had books and music printed in braille. In 1920 Helen helped found the American Civil Liberties Union (ACLU) to preserve the individual rights guaranteed to every person by the Constitution.

Helen was awarded the Presidential Medal of Freedom in 1964. This is one of the highest US civilian honors.

## "Although the world is full of suffering, it is full also of the overcoming of it."

### —Helen Keller

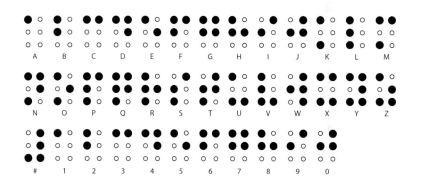

Braille: a writing system of raised dots that can be read with the fingers. Created by Louis Braille, who lost his sight at a young age, braille was inspired by Charles Barbier's "night-writing" code used in the military.

Helen Keller appears on the Alabama state quarter, first released on March 17, 2003.

Her name is in both English and braille.

Magnolia blossoms are on the right side.

ALABAMA
1819

HELEN KELLER

SPIRIT of COURAGE
NEN
2003
E PLURIBUS UNUM

The coin has a reeded, or grooved, edge. This security feature began when quarters were made of silver—to make sure no one filed off the edges to get some of the precious metal.

An Alabama longleaf pine branch is on the left side. The longleaf pine is the state tree.

In 1999 the US Mint began releasing a new quarter every ten weeks to honor each state. The front has an image of George Washington, while the back has a special state design. The quarters were released in the order each state entered the Union. The program ended in 2008.

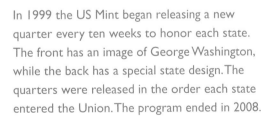

# Queen Sālote Tupou III
## Monarch • Peacemaker

From 1967 until 1974, banknotes featured Queen Sālote's portrait.

Queen Sālote was the first queen of Tonga. Tonga is located in the South Pacific and consists of 172 islands.

At age nine, Sālote was sent to school in New Zealand. She was there for five years.

Sālote was only considered as her father's heir because

| Born | March 13, 1900, in Tonga |
|------|--------------------------|
| Died | December 16, 1965, in New Zealand (65 years old) |

he didn't have any sons, and she was his only surviving daughter. She was married at age seventeen to the man whom many people wanted to be king, making the match popular. At age eighteen, after her father died, Salote became queen. Her husband became the prime minister.

During her reign, Queen Salote united Tonga, a feat no other Tongan chief had done. She worked to end the religious conflicts in her country. She also worked with authors and scholars to make a written account of the oral histories and genealogies of Tonga. As queen, she felt it was her duty to be the authority on the geneaology and traditions of her people.

The Tonga national coat of arms was designed in 1862. The three stars represent the three main groups of Tonga's islands, the crown symbolizes the kingdom of Tonga, the dove stands for peace, and the three swords are for Tonga's three royal dynasties. The motto means "From God and Tonga I descend."

The back of the two-pa'anga banknote shows women making tapa cloth.

Tapa cloth is made from bark that has been softened in water and then beaten by hand with a wood mallet. Designs are added with paints or vegetable dyes.

Tonga produces squash, coconuts, bananas, and vanilla beans.

A *ta'ovala*, a woven mat wrapped around the waist, is also worn on formal occasions.

Traditional dress in Tonga is the *tupenu*, a cloth wrapped around the waist similar to a sarong.

# Indira Gandhi
## Prime Minister • Politician

The former USSR put Indira on a commemorative stamp in 1984.

The Lion Capital of Ashoka was adopted as the official emblem of India in 1950. The sculpture has four Asiatic lions standing back-to-back on a base that includes other animals.

Indira Gandhi was the first, and to date only, female prime minister of India. She grew up in a political family. Her grandfather and parents were champions of Indian independence from Great Britain. Indira's mother was imprisoned in 1932

| Born | Indira Nehru on November 19, 1917, in Allahabad, India |
|------|--------------------------------------------------------|
| Died | October 31, 1984, in New Delhi, India (66 years old) |

for her part in a public campaign of civil disobedience. Her father became the first prime minister, which meant he was often away on government business. As an only child, Indira was lonely.

As she got older, Indira started to assist her father. She accompanied him on his travels as prime minister and slowly began her own political career. In January 1966, Indira became prime minister.

Indira held the role of prime minister for two terms. She was then voted out of office in 1977 after many people felt she abused her power. Indira ran for prime minister again and returned to power in 1980. During her time as prime minister, a program called the Green Revolution was started to increase food production. Indira was also the first government official to recognize the newly formed country of Bangladesh.

Before India became independent from Great Britain, Queen Victoria appeared on the front of India's coins.

**"You cannot shake hands with a clenched fist."**
**—Indira Gandhi**

Indira was featured on the five-rupee coin issued on her birthday, November 19, in 1985. This was the first time a five-rupee coin was minted.

Indira often wore a sari, a traditional women's garment made up of a length of cloth that is wrapped around the waist and draped over a shoulder.

Each mint has its own letter or symbol to identify where a coin is made, called a mintmark. The mintmark for the mint at Mumbai is a small diamond.

India is the world's second-largest producer of wheat and rice.

# Eva Perón

## Actress • First Lady • Activist

Eva is the first Argentine woman to be on a banknote, the one-hundred-peso note. It was unveiled on the sixtieth anniversary of her death, in July of 2012, and issued in September.

Eva's portrait is bordered by flowers from the ceibo tree, a symbol of the nation. Her birth and death dates are included. Below these dates is a quote from her: "As a woman I feel in my soul the warm tenderness of the town where I came from and to whom I owe myself."

Eva Perón is best known as the former First Lady of Argentina. Her rise to fame wasn't easy. Eva was one of five children raised by a single mother. She completed six years of school, but she didn't enjoy it.

Around age fifteen, Eva moved to Buenos Aires. She wanted to become an actress. She soon appeared in her first film and first radio drama. Eva later starred in a radio series where she performed biographies of famous women from history.

Eva married Juan Perón when she was twenty-four. He became president a year

| Born | María Eva Duarte on May 7, 1919, in Los Toldos, Argentina |
|---|---|
| Died | July 26, 1952, Buenos Aires, Argentina (33 years old) |
| Nickname | Evita |

later. As the First Lady, Eva promoted laws giving women the right to vote and worked to help the poor and to build schools.

She was so popular that the people wanted her to become vice president in Argentina's next election. Eva declined the nomination.

Ara Pacis Augustae, an altar in Rome to Pax, the goddess of peace, is shown on the left side of the back of the banknote. The words under the denomination say in Spanish that Eva was a popular leader who fought for the rights of workers and helped women gain the right to vote.

People who opposed the Perón government wanted to bury Eva in an unmarked grave, so Perón supporters sent her body to Europe for safekeeping. Eva's body returned to Argentina twenty-six years after her death. Eva was laid to rest in the Duarte family tomb, and her sister has the only key.

Eva was also featured on the one-peso and fifty-centavos coins in 1997, the fiftieth anniversary of her death.

Evita City is a suburb of Buenos Aires founded in 1947 by President Juan Perón to honor Eva. It is shaped to look like Eva's profile.

# The Mirabal Sisters

## Revolutionaries • Icons • Martyrs

The Mirabal sisters are known for resisting Rafael Trujillo of the Dominican Republic, a dictator, or a ruler with absolute power.

Though they grew up in a rural town, their mother wanted them to have an education. What they learned in Catholic boarding school opened their eyes to the injustices of the dictatorship. They realized how much of their daily life it controlled. Patria had been interested in becoming a nun, but she joined the revolution to fight for justice and peace. Minerva wanted to be a revolutionary. She also wanted to be a lawyer. Her studies were interrupted when she was placed under house arrest for three

| Patria | |
|---|---|
| Born | February 27, 1924 |
| Died | November 25, 1960 (36 years old) |
| **Minerva** | |
| Born | March 12, 1927 |
| Died | November 25, 1960 (33 years old) |
| **María Teresa** | |
| Born | October 15, 1936 |
| Died | November 25, 1960 (25 years old) |
| The sisters were born in Salcedo, Dominican Republic, and died in the Dominican Republic | |

years, but she eventually finished her law degree and graduated with the highest honors. Minerva was arrested three times during her life. María Teresa wanted to be rid of the evil Trujillo.

The three sisters helped organize a group called the "Movement of the Fourteenth of June" to oppose Trujillo. They recruited members and took action by handing out leaflets, holding meetings, and spreading news of the abuse of the Trujillo regime.

In 1997 a 137-foot refurbished obelisk—a four-sided momument with a pyramid-like shape at the top—was unveiled in Santo Domingo, the capital of the Dominican Republic. The obelisk is covered with images of the Mirabal sisters.

The three Mirabal sisters are shown on the 200-peso note issued in 2007. There is a butterfly with them because they were nicknamed "Las Mariposas" ("The Butterflies").

The reverse side shows a monument to the sisters in Salcedo, near their childhood home. There is a glossy security stripe on the back of the bill that appears golden only when the bill is flat.

A Dominican postage stamp of the Mirabal sisters was issued on December 19, 1985.

The Mirabal sisters are honored each year on November 25. The United Nations dedicated this day as the International Day for the Elimination of Violence Against Women in honor of the Mirabal sisters.

# Britannia
## Symbol of a Nation

In the second century, the Greeks often used a female figure to represent a city or country. Her features and clothing were symbolic of that place.

Britannia is one such symbol.

She's been depicted on coins since the first century, when she was represented as a goddess. In the second century, the Romans created a coin where Britannia is shown in the Greek art style wearing the traditional dress: a short tunic, boots, and a cloak. Her spear in her hand and the shield on the ground near her suggest military vigilance. The rocks under her right foot represent the geographical features of northern Britain.

After the British Isles became independent from the Roman Empire, Britannia became a symbol of unity and strength for Great Britain. When the Bank of England first issued coins in the late 1600s, Britannia was depicted with a spear and an olive branch.

During the 1700s, Britannia symbolized British pride as a sea power. She is shown sitting on rocks with ships in the background, holding a trident rather than a spear.

In 2008 the British government decided to stop featuring Britannia on currency. For the first time in 336 years, she didn't appear on a new coin.

*Britannia* is a Latin word meaning "a collection of islands with different names."

Britannia first appeared on Roman coins in about 119 CE.

British currency first depicted Britannia in 1672—fourteen centuries after she was shown on Roman coins. This version of Britannia holds an olive sprig in her right hand to symbolize peace.

This version of Britannia was on the twopenny and penny, the first coins minted on a steam-powered machine. The coins were large and heavy—the twopenny weighed two ounces and the penny weighed an ounce.

SCOTLAND

N. IRELAND

REPUBLIC OF IRELAND

ENGLAND

WALES

# Lady Liberty
## Symbol of Freedom • Towering Statue

Like Britannia represents Great Britain, Lady Liberty represents the United States. She stands for freedom, peace, and sometimes military power. The best-known depiction of her might be the Statue of Liberty in New York Harbor. But Lady Liberty has been on currency since it was first minted in the United States in 1792.

The figure of Lady Liberty with a cap on top of a pole was used as a symbol of freedom during the American Revolution.

Her image has changed over the years. When she was first introduced on coins in 1794, Lady Liberty's head of flowing hair took up most of the space. These coins are rare; one sold for more than $10 million dollars in 2013.

On the 1836 silver dollar coin, Lady Liberty still has her flowing hair, but now she's sitting on a rock. This is often referred to as the Gobrecht dollar, after the engraver, Christian Gobrecht. The pole in her left hand with the liberty cap on top represent freedom. The union shield in her right hand represents Congress and the thirteen original colonies.

The Walking Liberty half dollar of the early 1900s shows Lady Liberty standing. The laurel and oak branches she holds symbolize the military. Her arm is held out to represent sharing liberty with others.

The Lady Liberty coin issued in 2017 shows her as African American for the first time. This coin commemorates the 225th anniversary of the US Mint opening and is made of almost 100 percent 24-karat gold.

The face of Lady Liberty appeared on every US coin for more than one hundred years.

# Author's Note

Even today, most individuals chosen to be put on a coin or bill are men. Few women have received this honor: those who overcame obstacles, broke barriers, and achieved greatness. Now they all share a common legacy of being on money.

In the United States, there are plans for Harriet Tubman to replace Andrew Jackson on the twenty-dollar bill. She will be the first African American woman to be featured on a bill and the first woman on a US bill in more than one hundred years.

Women have historically been overlooked for their achievements, accomplishments, and activism, so their appearance on currency is all the more special. Money is essential to our daily lives, and highlighting these women on our coins and bills reminds us to remember and celebrate them and leads us to wonder who will be deserving of the honor in the future.

# Glossary

**BCE (Before the Common Era):** the common era begins in year one in the Gregorian calendar, which is used throughout the world today.

**Bureau of Engraving and Printing:** handles the creation and circulation of paper money in the U.S. The Bureau prints more than 750 million dollars worth of paper money each day.

**coat of arms:** a group of pictures or symbols representing a country, family, or person.

**euro:** the official currency of nineteen out of twenty-eight member countries of the European union. The euro was introduced in the late 1990s and can be used in any of the nineteen European nations. The euro banknotes don't highlight national figures but represent unity through bridges, windows, arches, flags, and a map of Europe.

**mint:** a factory where coins are made. The mintmark on a coin tells where it was produced. In the United States, the letter *D* is the mintmark for the Denver Mint and the letter *P* is the mintmark for the Philadelphia Mint.